COUNTRY  PROFILES

# THAILAND

BY EMILY ROSE OACHS

BELLWETHER MEDIA • MINNEAPOLIS, MN

**Blastoff! Discovery** launches a new mission: reading to learn. Filled with facts and features, each book offers you an exciting new world to explore!

This edition first published in 2018 by Bellwether Media, Inc.

No part of this publication may be reproduced in whole or in part without written permission of the publisher.
For information regarding permission, write to Bellwether Media, Inc.,
Attention: Permissions Department,
5357 Penn Avenue South, Minneapolis, MN 55419.

Library of Congress Cataloging-in-Publication Data

Names: Oachs, Emily Rose, author.
Title: Thailand / by Emily Rose Oachs.
Description: Minneapolis, MN : Bellwether Media, Inc., 2018. |
    Series: Blastoff! Discovery: Country Profiles | Includes bibliographical
    references and index. | Audience: Grades 3-8.
Identifiers: LCCN 2017034070 (print) | LCCN 2017035255 (ebook)
    | ISBN 9781626177369 (hardcover : alk. paper) | ISBN
    9781681034904 (ebook)
Subjects:  LCSH: Thailand–Juvenile literature.
Classification: LCC DS563.5 (ebook) | LCC DS563.5 .O23 2018
    (print) | DDC 959.3–dc23
LC record available at https://lccn.loc.gov/2017034070

Editor: Paige V. Polinsky     Designer: Brittany McIntosh

Printed in the United States of America, North Mankato, MN.

# TABLE OF CONTENTS

WAT MAHATHAT

Early in the morning, a couple of visitors bike toward Sukhothai Historical Park in northwestern Thailand. Hundreds of years ago, Thailand was called the Kingdom of Siam. Sukhothai was its busy capital city. Today, only ruins remain of ancient Sukhothai.

## OTHER TOP SITES

DAMNOEN SADUAK
FLOATING MARKET

GRAND PALACE

KHAO YAI
NATIONAL PARK

WAT PHO

The visitors pass peaceful ponds dotted with floating lotus flowers. Soon, magnificent Buddhist temples, or *wats*, come into view. They are all decorated with **elegant** carvings. But Wat Si Chum stands out from the rest. The visitors park their bikes and step through its entrance. Inside, they find a 49-foot (15-meter) statue of the seated Buddha. This is Thailand!

MYANMAR (BURMA)

Thailand is a country in southeastern Asia. It spreads across 198,117 square miles (513,120 square kilometers). Bangkok, Thailand's capital, rests near the **Gulf** of Thailand on the southern coast.

The Mekong River separates eastern Thailand from Laos. Cambodia lies to Thailand's southeast, while Myanmar forms the country's western border. A narrow arm of land reaches south from western Thailand. This **peninsula** stands between the Gulf of Thailand in the east and the Andaman Sea to the west. Several hundred islands dot this long coastline. Malaysia meets Thailand at the far southern tip.

ANDAMAN SEA

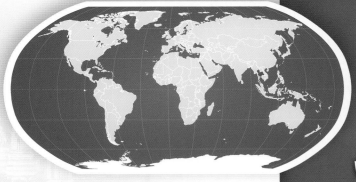

N
W E
S

CHIANG
MAI

LAOS

UDON
THANI

MEKONG
RIVER

THAILAND

NONTHABURI

BANGKOK

SAMUT
PRAKAN

CAMBODIA

GULF
OF THAILAND

## A SLIM STRETCH

Thailand is just 8 miles
(13 kilometers) across at
its narrowest point!

HAT YI

MALAYSIA

Low, forested mountains cover much of northern Thailand. They stretch south along the country's western border. The Khorat **Plateau** lies in the northeast. Between the mountains and plateau, **plains** spread across central Thailand. The Chao Phraya River flows through this region. Mountains, forests, and sandy beaches mark Thailand's southern peninsula.

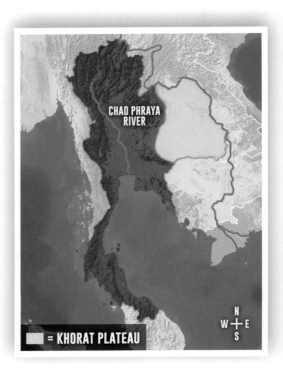

CHAO PHRAYA RIVER

☐ = KHORAT PLATEAU

N
W + E
S

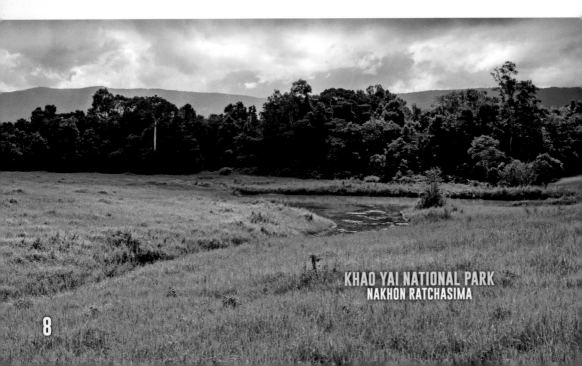

**KHAO YAI NATIONAL PARK**
NAKHON RATCHASIMA

KO LANTA

**BANGKOK**

Average
seasonal highs
and lows

**JANUARY**
HIGH: 89 °F (32 °C)
LOW: 71 °F (22 °C)

**APRIL**
HIGH: 94 °F (34 °C)
LOW: 80 °F (27 °C)

**JULY**
HIGH: 90 °F (32 °C)
LOW: 78 °F (26 °C)

**OCTOBER**
HIGH: 89 °F (32 °C)
LOW: 77 °F (25 °C)

°F = degrees Fahrenheit
°C = degrees Celsius

Thailand's climate is hot and **tropical**. The rainy season brings **monsoons** from May through October. Between November and February, the air is cool and dry. Higher elevations keep northern Thailand cooler than the south.

**Deforestation** has harmed many of Thailand's **habitats**. But Thai **nature reserves** are helping to bring wildlife back. **Endangered** Asian elephants rumble through the forested mountains of western Thailand. A falling number of tigers still stalk deer and wild boars in that region. Malayan sun bears also dine on termites and honey among the trees.

Gibbons and macaques swing through the branches of Thailand's tropical forests. Brightly colored trogons and great hornbills build their nests throughout the country. In **mangrove forests**, water monitor lizards hunt for birds, snakes, and other small animals. Siamese crocodiles lurk in the waters of Thailand's rivers.

INDOCHINESE TIGER

TROGON

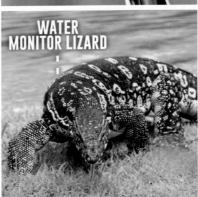

WATER MONITOR LIZARD

SIAMESE CROCODILE

LAR GIBBON

# ASIAN ELEPHANT

Life Span: up to 60 years
Red List Status: endangered

Asian elephant range =

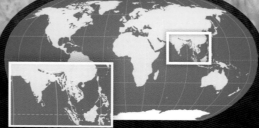

| LEAST CONCERN | NEAR THREATENED | VULNERABLE | ENDANGERED | CRITICALLY ENDANGERED | EXTINCT IN THE WILD | EXTINCT |
|---|---|---|---|---|---|---|

**PEOPLE**

## PROUD TO BE FREE

Many Thai call their country the "land of the free." They are proud that it never fell under European control. Thailand has always been independent!

About 68 million people live in Thailand. Most of the country's occupants are Thai. Some have **ancestors** from China or Malaysia. A small number of Thai citizens moved there from Myanmar.

Thai is the nation's official and most common language. In Thai, one word can mean different things. The meaning changes based on the speaker's tone! Many people also speak English, which is often used in business. Almost all Thai people practice Buddhism. Around Bangkok and the southern peninsula, small numbers follow Islam.

## FAMOUS FACE

**Name:** Sombat "Buakaw" Banchamek
**Birthday:** May 8, 1982
**Hometown:** Ban Ko Kaeo, Thailand
**Famous for:** World champion Muay Thai fighter, kickboxer, and actor in two Thai action movies

## SPEAK THAI

Thai uses characters instead of letters. However, Thai words can be written with the English alphabet so you can read them.

CHIANG MAI

| ENGLISH | THAI | HOW TO SAY IT |
|---------|------|---------------|
| hello | sawatdee | sah-waht-DEE |
| goodbye | jer gan | gehr GAHN |
| please | kor | KAHR |
| thank you | kob-khun | kawb-KOON |
| yes | chai | CHAI |
| no | mai-chai | my-CHAI |

## COMMUNITIES

Thai families are very busy. They often have little time to spend together between work and school. Still, family is important to the Thai. Several generations may share a home. The children frequently live with their parents until they are married or have found jobs. As parents age, their grown children are expected to care for them.

*TUK-TUKS* IN BANGKOK

PHANG NGA
BAY

Countryside villages are home to about half of Thailand's population. A wat stands in each village. Some village families still dwell in **traditional** raised houses built on stilts. In cities, families usually live in small apartments. Motorcycle taxis, three-wheeled *tuk-tuks*, and buses carry people from place to place. Paved roads and trains connect much of the country.

15

*WAI*

## LOWLY FEET

Thai believe the feet are unclean. People must not touch others with their feet or show the soles of their feet to others. This is considered very rude!

To greet others, Thai perform the *wai*. The person of lower status bows with palms pressed together at the chest. Then the other person repeats it back. The wai can also be used as a thank-you or goodbye. Performing it shows respect.

Buddhism plays a central role in Thai daily life. In Thai homes, many families display statues of Buddha and burn **incense**. Traditionally, young men serve as Buddhist **monks** for a short period. This time is taken very seriously. But Thai people also value *sanuk*, or fun and humor. They work to find pleasure in even the smallest pieces of everyday life.

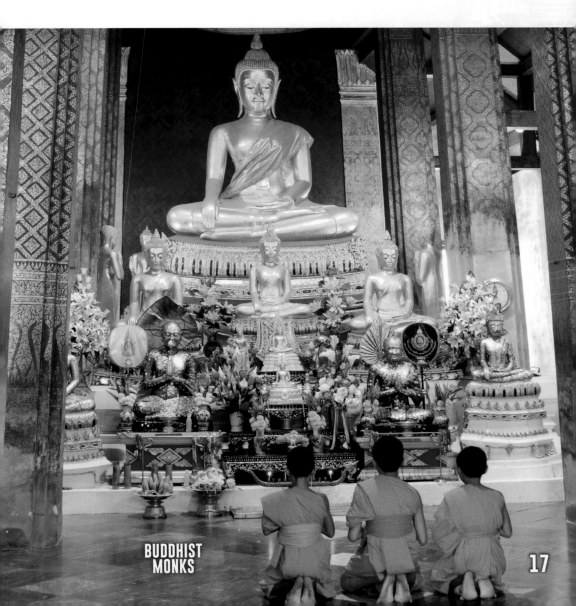

BUDDHIST
MONKS

The Thai government offers free public education through secondary school. Children must enter school at age 6. They are required to attend six years of primary school, followed by three years of secondary school. After, some receive training for jobs. Others prepare for university.

Most Thai hold **service jobs**. They may work in shops, hospitals, or schools. Farming employs about three out of ten Thai workers. Rice is the country's main crop and a key **export**. Farmers grow much of it in Thailand's central plains. Other common crops include coconuts, mangoes, and sugarcane.

NURSE

RICE FARMING

MUAY THAI

Thailand's national sport is *Muay Thai*, or Thai kickboxing. During matches, live bands play *sarama*, fighting music, beside the ring. Another popular sport is *takraw*. It features a small woven ball. Players must use any body part but their hands or arms to keep it from striking the ground.

TAKRAW

Many Thai enjoy playing *makruk*, a chess-like board game. Some practice the traditional Thai art of fruit carving. They carve detailed shapes into melons, apples, and more. Shopping is another popular pastime. Friends explore busy markets and shopping malls together.

FRUIT CARVING

# PAPER KRATHONG

During the celebration of *Loy Krathong,* Thai people make small boats shaped like lotus blossoms. They float these *krathong* on water to get rid of bad luck and wish for good!

## What You Need:
- cardboard
- cup or bowl (for tracing)
- colorful construction paper
- pencil
- scissors
- glue
- coins, fresh flowers (optional)

## Instructions:
1. Trace two circles onto the cardboard. Cut them out.

2. Cut the remaining cardboard into the shape of a lotus petal.

3. Trace the petal shape onto the construction paper. Cut it out. Repeat until you have about 16 or enough to arrange two layers of petals around a cardboard circle.

4. Glue the petals around the edge of one circle. Then, glue on another layer of petals overlapping the first. Glue the second circle on top.

5. Roll the first layer of petals forward so their tips point toward the center. Roll the second layer of petals back, pointing their tips outward.

6. Cut a thin strip of paper. Then cut fringe along its long side. Glue this strip into a circle around the center of your lotus. If you have coins or fresh flowers, place them inside the fringed ring. Happy Loy Krathong!

Thai food is known for being sweet, sour, and spicy. Fish sauce and chilies are common ingredients. Fresh herbs like basil and lemongrass also make dishes flavorful. Rice is served with most meals. Between meals, snacking is popular. Street carts sell snacks of tropical fruits and *satay*, or meat grilled on a stick.

Thai people often eat dinner family style. They share dishes of food around the table. A popular meal is green curry, a stew made with coconut milk, green chilies, and meats. People often pair grilled chicken with spicy *som tam*, a green papaya salad. Dessert may be sticky rice with fresh mango.

GREEN CURRY

SOM TAM

## MANGO STICKY RICE RECIPE

**Ingredients:**
water for soaking rice
1 1/2 cups sticky rice
2 cups water
1 cup coconut milk
1 teaspoon salt
6 tablespoons brown sugar
3 ripe mangoes, sliced

**Steps:**

1. Place the rice into a bowl and cover with water. Allow the rice to soak. After at least 4 hours, drain the rice.

2. With an adult present, use a steamer to cook the rice. This should take about 15 to 20 minutes.

3. In a pot, have an adult help you mix the coconut milk, salt, and sugar together over medium heat and bring to a boil. Stir until the mixture is smooth.

4. Slowly combine half of the mixture with the cooked rice. Stir together and let sit for at least an hour.

5. Scoop rice into a bowl. Arrange the mango slices on top. Serve the remaining coconut mixture on the side. Enjoy!

# CELEBRATIONS

Many of Thailand's major holidays are Buddhist celebrations. *Visakha Puja* is the holiest of the Buddhist holidays. It honors the life of Buddha. People gather at their wats for sermons and **rituals**.

The holiday *Khao Phansa* stretches from July to October. Monks spend it **meditating** and **fasting**. Colorful festivals with candles and flowers mark Khao Phansa Day, the start of this period. In mid-April, Thai celebrate *Songkran*, the lunar New Year. During this celebration, people spray water and toss flour onto others to bring good luck. This bright, playful holiday shows Thailand's love of sanuk!

SONGKRAN

# LUCKY LANTERNS

In northern Thailand's Chiang Mai, Loy Krathong is known as the Yee Peng Festival. There, Thai release hundreds of floating lanterns into the sky.

**1296**
City of Chiang Mai built

**1868**
King Chulalongkorn, a powerful and popular king, begins his rule

**1238 CE**
Thailand becomes independent from Khmer rulers

**900s BCE**
Mon and Khmer kingdoms formed in the region of modern Thailand

**1932**
The Siamese Revolution turns Thailand into a constitutional monarchy

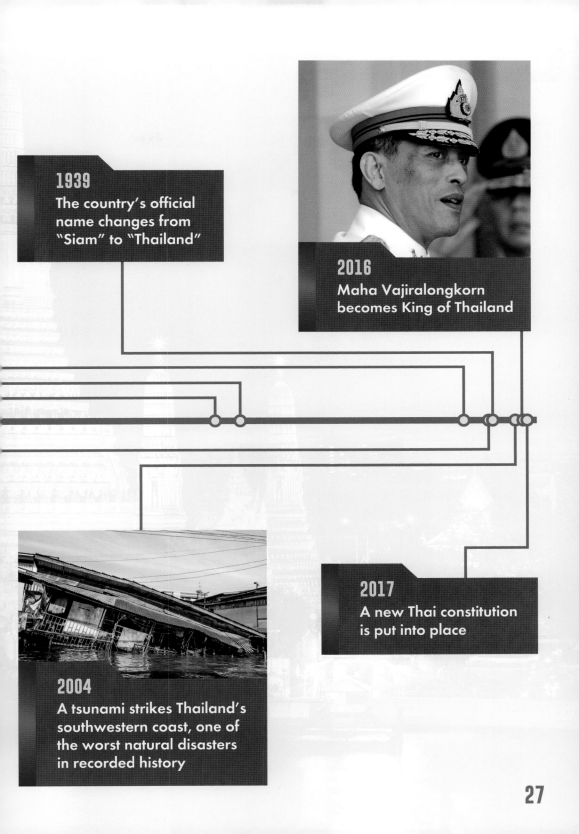

**1939**
The country's official name changes from "Siam" to "Thailand"

**2016**
Maha Vajiralongkorn becomes King of Thailand

**2017**
A new Thai constitution is put into place

**2004**
A tsunami strikes Thailand's southwestern coast, one of the worst natural disasters in recorded history

# THAILAND FACTS

**Official Name:** Kingdom of Thailand

**Flag of Thailand:** Thailand's flag features five horizontal stripes. A thick horizontal blue band goes across the center of the flag. Narrow white stripes run above and below it. Red stripes stand along the flag's top and bottom borders. The blue stands for Thailand's king and monarchy. The white represents the Buddhist religion, while the red stripes are symbols of blood shed for the country. Thailand adopted this flag in 1917.

**Area:** 198,117 square miles
(513,120 square kilometers)

**Capital City:** Bangkok

**Important Cities:** Samut Prakan, Udon Thani, Nonthaburi, Chiang Mai, Hat Yi

**Population:**
68,414,135 (July 2017)

**WHERE PEOPLE LIVE**

COUNTRYSIDE
**47.3%**

CITY
**52.7%**

**MANUFACTURING**
**16.7%**

JOBS

**FARMING**
**31.8%**

**SERVICES**
**51.5%**

**Main Exports:**

vehicles    electronics    rice

computers    gems

**National Holiday:**
Birthday of King Maha
Vajiralongkorn (July 28)

**Main Languages:**
Thai, Burmese

**Form of Government:**
constitutional monarchy

**Title for Country Leaders:**
king, prime minister

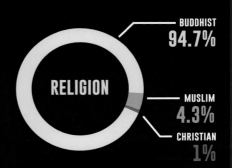

**BUDDHIST**
**94.7%**

RELIGION

**MUSLIM**
**4.3%**

**CHRISTIAN**
**1%**

**Unit of Money:**
Thai baht; 100 satang equal one baht.

# GLOSSARY

**ancestors**—relatives who lived long ago

**deforestation**—the clearing of forests

**elegant**—of a high quality

**endangered**—at risk of becoming extinct

**export**—a product sold by one country to another

**fasting**—choosing not to eat

**gulf**—part of an ocean or sea that extends into land

**habitats**—lands with certain types of plants, animals, and weather

**incense**—long, thin sticks of material that smell pleasant when burned

**mangrove forests**—thick tropical forests that can grow along coasts in salty swamp water

**meditating**—quietly thinking or reflecting for religious purposes or relaxation

**monks**—men who have given up all their belongings to become part of a specific religious community

**monsoons**—winds that shift direction each season; monsoons bring heavy rain.

**nature reserves**—areas where animals and other natural resources are protected

**peninsula**—a section of land that extends out from a larger piece of land and is almost completely surrounded by water

**plains**—large areas of flat land

**plateau**—an area of flat, raised land

**rituals**—religious ceremonies or practices

**service jobs**—jobs that perform tasks for people or businesses

**traditional**—related to customs, ideas, or beliefs handed down from one generation to the next

**tropical**—part of the tropics; the tropics is a hot, rainy region near the equator.

# TO LEARN MORE

## AT THE LIBRARY
Friedman, Mel. *Thailand*. New York, N.Y.:
Children's Press, 2015.

Marsico, Katie. *Buddhism*. Ann Arbor, Mich.:
Cherry Lake Publishing, 2017.

VeLure Roholt, Christine. *Foods of Thailand*.
Minneapolis, Minn.: Bellwether Media, 2014.

## ON THE WEB

Learning more about Thailand
is as easy as 1, 2, 3.

1. Go to www.factsurfer.com.

2. Enter "Thailand" into the search box.

3. Click the "Surf" button and you will see a list of
   related web sites.

With factsurfer.com, finding more information is just
a click away.

# INDEX

The images in this book are reproduced through the courtesy of: Sarawut Chamsaeng, front cover; Anekoho, pp. 4-5; Top Ten 22 Photo, p. 5 (top); Bule Sky Studio, p. 5 (middle top); Casper1774 Studio, p. 5 (middle bottom); Juan Martinez, p. 5 (bottom); Brittany McIntosh, pp. 6-7, 8 (inset); Sasha 64F, p. 8; Kuttig - Travel - 2/ Alamy, p. 9; TW Stock, p. 9 (inset); May Chanikran, p. 10 (top); Noicherry Beans, p. 10 (middle top); Nana Trongratanawong, p. 10 (middle bottom); Puwadol Jaturawuttichai, p. 10 (bottom left); M Massel, p. 10 (bottom right); TDee Photo CM, pp. 10-11; Anekoho, p. 12; Tofudevil, p. 13 (top); 501 Room, p. 13 (bottom); FotoTrav, p. 14; Jan Wlodarczyk/ Alamy, p. 15; Jaboo2Foto, p. 16; Happy Dancing, p. 17; Bruchuda BoonPlien, p. 18; Toey Toey, p. 19 (top); Ruchuda Boonplien, p. 19 (bottom); PhotoFriday, p. 20 (top); Pal2ityawit, p. 20 (bottom); suchart seehamart, p. 21 (top); Tamara Peterson, p. 21 (bottom); Sorbis, p. 22; Pepsee30, p. 23 (top); Tortoon, p. 23 (middle); Tong4130, p. 23 (bottom); View Apart, pp. 24 (inset), 27 (bottom); AdisomFoto, pp. 24-25; Alan Bauman, p. 26; PKittiwongsakul, p. 27 (top); Mtkang, p. 29 (currency); Shaynepplstockphoto, p. 29 (coin, top); Watcharapong Saiboot, p. 29 (coin, bottom).